Judges
And
An
Angel
Rule On Possibilities

We Can Cut Sentences &
Prison Costs

Reverend Mike Wanner

Table Of Contents

Introduction

Some sources report that in America alone there are more that 2.3 million people in jail.

I like most people was totally oblivious to that fact. I started channeling Angel Raphael in 2013 and started releasing little message sets at they came through.

In message set 16 of the Angel Raphael Speaks Series there was a message

"I asked Mike to Step in to Prison Energetically

I have asked Mike to get the address and location within a prison of a designated space so he can visit energetically and receive feedback for us. Whether he will have time, interest or opportunity to do this will be interesting to see. As he writes this, he is not thrilled with the idea. We are already consuming a lot of his time."   ARS16

I had resisted that invitation to visit jail energetically until 2016.

1 - Why I am Writing This Book

The invitation that I referenced just above was finally embraced in 2016. So far, The Angel Raphael prodding has had me publish the following books related to prisons:

1. *Angel Raphael Speaks Volume 4: Angels, Addicts, Alcoholics & Prisoners – Oh Yeah!*
2. *Angel Raphael Speaks Volume 5:* Prisoners Caring for Alcoholics - Australia In Miniature Projects Intro
3. *Angel Raphael Speaks Volume 6:* Prisoners Caring for Addicts - Australia In Miniature For Addicts
4. *Prison Jobs Now: Providing Care For Addicts And   Alcoholics*
5. *Angel Raphael Speaks - Prisons* (A Kindle only book -2013)
6. *Contained Care Communities Concept*
7. *Australia In Miniature*
8. *Prison Possibilities Dialogue Series: Concept*
9. *Prison Possibilities Dialogue Series: Volume 2 Dialogues*
10. *Prison Possibilities Dialogue Series: Volume 3 Dialogues*
11. *Prison Possibilities Dialogue Series: Volume 4 Dialogues*
12. *Prison Possibilities Dialogue Series: Volume 5 Dialogues*
13. *Prison Possibilities Voluntary Exile: Concept*
14. *Prison Possibilities Correction Coaches: Concept*
15. *Prison Possibilities for Mexicans: Is A Boat Better than A Wall?*
16. *Prison Possibilities Family Time:* A Reason to Thrive!
17. Prison Genius Pool: *"So Much Genius In Jail"*
18. *Prison Possibilities Access Systems: Prisoner Access by Request*
19. *Prisoner's Lawyers Can Save The American Economy: Make A Buck Doing It & Be Thanked!*
20. *Prisoner Family Talks, Days, Stays & Vacations: Connecting Helps Healing*
21. *Prisoner Writing Projects: Write To Heal, Start Over & Reconnect*
22. *Prison Cell Clearing & Blessing: Clear Entities, Chase Ghosts, and & Create Sacred Space*
23. *Prisoner Professors*
24. *Prison Reiki? Maybe Someday? A Gateway To Help Heal Prisons & America?*

This book continues to carry potential for rethinking that can help to reduce incarceration to those who we need there.

2 - Disclaimer

I, the author, am not involved with prisons or prisoners but I have talked to many prisoners during Hospital Pastoral Visitations. I am sharing what is coming to me in an effort to spread understanding and trigger conversation that can be helpful. It may be that the discussion needs finessing and I invite your wisdom in the mix.

My guidance has suggested that a lot can be done. I will detail my views which are not the expert positions of a Corrections Officer or Corrections Administrator or Corrections Manager or Corrections Supervisor, or Medical Practitioner or Psychologist or Psychiatrist or Social Worker or other expert who might be helpful here.

As I have said many times before, everything that I look at about prisons seems to be so complicated. Here I suggest some things that have come to my awareness regarding United States Sentencing Commission 2010 Judges Survey that align with channeled messages from Angel Raphael.

Note

I have written five books titled Prison Possibilities Dialogue Series and I invite submissions in the format specified. The core message about the series can be found for free at http://angelraphaelspeaks.com/prison-possibilities/

I invite the consideration of the matter herein and opinions to further dialogue and progress.

3 - Why Would A Federal Judge Quit

There is a report in the news about a Federal Judge in Nashville who left the bench because he was uncomfortable living up to the duty of silence that comes with the robe. This got my attention because you do not hear about something like that very often.

It seems that mandatory minimum sentences had an impact on a case before the judge. The law required that the defendant be sentenced to life imprisonment.

Taking the robe off and resigning removed the duty to be quiet. The ex-judge could then go public with a declaration of his dissatisfaction with his duty to sentence the prisoner to life.

The Tennessean denounced mandatory minimum sentences. Of course, the statement did not influence the sentence that had been made that the prisoner is still serving now.

The Judge Is Not Alone

The story got my attention so I did some googling and was very surprised at what I found. In the chapters below you will find some answers that I found interesting.

When more than 50% of the judges said that some mandatory minimum sentences should be delinked, That seemed like a strong indication to me that we have work to do.

4 - Judging Must be Extremely Difficult

It seems that the judges are in an almost impossible situation. Somebody will be very upset with every decision that is made.

Sentencing has to be very difficult for each Judge each time. They are speaking for the people in the jurisdiction that has placed them on the bench

In America alone, there are more that 2.3 million people in jail including roughly some 1,351,000 state prisoners in some 1,710+ state prisons, 211,000+ federal prisoners in 100+ federal prisons and 34,000 youth prisoners in 940+ juvenile correctional facilities and some 646,000 local prisoners in some 3,280+ local and tribal jails.

The judges that convicted the prisoners made hard choices and did what the citizens required of them. I do not envy them their jobs.

The job requires them to represent society and determine how society will treat those who have been accused of breaking the law. The judge may also be charged with teaching the law to a jury if one is needed, interpreting how the law applies to the specific case, maintaining order in the presentation of the facts, counseling legal representatives on appropriate legal presentations and insuring fairness.

Each case before a judge is unique in some manner and it is necessary to identify every aspect that is comparable to statutes and case law and also identify circumstances that are not comparable so that the record reflects the interpretation.

Observers may not be able to believe their eyes and their ears at times because that which they see in the courtroom may be radically different than their expectation. There is not one set of laws that applies to everybody in every court throughout the nation.

There are many states, cities, regions, authorities, tribes, military groups and municipal courts throughout the nation that can have laws, rules and statutes that are different than their neighboring authorities. While federal law or guidelines may be superior in some ways, the presiding judge needs to determine the applicable law.

Law is not the only factor for the judge to consider or a jury if there is one. Evidence and human dynamics of the defendants and witnesses must also be evaluated in the proceedings to determine the appropriateness of the evidence or testimony.

It may be that there is some impairment of the defendant that needs to be professionally evaluated. A report that I read from Casa Columbia at Columbia University declared, "65% of All U.S. Inmates Meet Medical Criteria for Substance Abuse Addiction,…" New York, N.Y., February 26, 2010

All the above has been stated to establish that Judges do not have an easy job and they have to be decisive in order to establish the kind of balance that we need in our society to keep things functioning and fair. Since they are doing the deciding every day, It would be wise if our society heard them clearly.

Their Survey answers follow. Please Consider their views.

"Congress should amend 18 USC § 3553(e) to authorize judges to sentence a defendant below the applicable statutory mandatory minimum to reflect a defendant's substantial assistance, even if the government does not make a motion."

Answered by 633 Abstain - 6

Two Largest Answers Total 54% Agree

Strongly Agree 25%

Somewhat Agree 29%

"The Commission should amend USSG §5K1.1 to authorize judges to sentence below the applicable guideline range to reflect a defendant's substantial assistance, even if the government does not make a motion.

Answered by 632 Abstain - 7

Two Largest Answers Total 54% Agree

Strongly Agree 25%

Somewhat Agree 29%

"The Federal Rules of Criminal Procedure should be amended to authorize judges to reduce a defendant's sentence under Rule 35(b) if the defendant, after sentencing, provides the required assistance, even if the government does not make a motion."

Answered by 633 Abstain - 6

Two Largest Answers Total 48% Agree

Strongly Agree 22%

Somewhat Agree 26%

"The Commission should amend USSG §5K1.1 to provide additional guidance regarding the extent to which a court may depart under that provision (*i.e.*, provide specific guidance on the number of offense levels recommended for departures based on the factors enumerated in USSG§5K1.1).

Answered by 630 Abstain - 9

Two Largest Answers Total 42% Agree

Strongly Agree 14%

Somewhat Agree 28%

9 - The Best People to Recommend Change

The message from the judges seems clear but who is listening? I wonder! They have shared their opinions but that really changes nothing in the present or near future.

I reflect on the complexity of the system and the intricate procedures needed to start the process. Opinions don't change laws but they can be the start of a movement that can move in the direction that will end in change.

Complexity at every step and risk for those who take the initiative toward change. The risk may be political, economic, personal, professional, family centered, community centered or be just to time intensive for most folks to fit in to their lives.

The last paragraph was written to promote the awareness of the reality that change will not come easily or without sacrifice for those who seek it.

If you would like to see things change, it is unlikely that you will be able to incentivize that happening by yourself. You could get frustrated and miserable by yourself but that will help nobody else or you.

There are 501C3 Non-Profit organizations trying to help change the dynamics. You could help them to further changes in the system and find a support community in the process.

I suggest that you might choose appropriate agencies that can match you interests and serve those who you are concerned about. Best wishes for success.

10 - Angel Raphael Spoke Earlier

In 2013, I published the first fourteen messages from the Angel Raphael Series that were directed to the prison situation. They were published as a Single Topic Message Set Titled *Angel Raphael Speaks – Prisons* on Kindle and also included in *Angel Raphael Speaks Volume One* on Amazon.

I invite you to notice the coincidence of the 50% Judges perspective on sentencing and the Angel Raphael 47% saving possibility. Radical shifts like that could dramatically increase the funding for quality of life programs in America.

The coincidence of such a radical shift from the wise judges and Angel Raphael are of particular interest to me because I respect all of them and healing is needed.

I will post below the messages from Angel Raphael that came before so that readers can understand a little better. I did not want to get in to this conversation but I was invited as I channeled Angel Raphael and now it all makes sense.

The messages below will be :
- Introduction from the Angel Raphael Speaks E-book
- Speaking from Prison Message from ARS 8
- Prison Life of the Future from ARS 9
- Prison Rehabilitation from ARS 10
- 47% Decrease in Per Prisoner Costs

I am hopeful that a new level or revitalization and understanding awaits us all and brings with it a whole new level of possibilities for America.

11 - "Introduction

I would like to dedicate this e-book to the Prison Ministry of Reverend Marion McGowan. Reverend Marion is a Circle Of Miracles Minister who was consulting with me about the time that the Angel Raphael Series started.

I was absolutely amazed that Angel Raphael picked up on the conversation and had so much to say. After the third writing, it became clear that this was an area that Angel Raphael really wanted to be developed for the greater good of the societies of many nations. I have brought together parts of e-books 8, 9, 10, and 11 to bring the topic writings into this format.

The channeling about prisons was making less sense to me than anything prior. I was amazed and confused because the channeling was different in that I usually heard messages in my head first and took them down. With some prison messages, I was not hearing but my fingers were typing.

After reading all the pieces, it makes so much sense to spend the government money on building success for programs and a reduction in recidivism. It would be so delightful if humane treatment of prisoners could lead to a scenario where correctional institution actually rehabbed lives by promoting the genius of criminal minds to be redirected to prison savings, reduction in violence and an opportunity for real revitalization. I sincerely hope that open-minded government leaders hear the ideas and take action.   *Reverend Mike* "

12 - "Speaking from Prison

It is good that you can hear Rev. Marion as she does not feel heard by the many. She does hear those who are restricted to the penal system and she hears them like you do her.

She listens to the truth that they cannot speak because they have been brought up in a society that dismissed their humanity before their spark of genius had an opportunity to shine. She has a message of love that says simply that they are each loved and let us together open to the possibilities for your gift to the world.

The absence of love in the lives of the imprisoned congregation she serves is the fertile field from which grew the human weeds of thinking that stifled all goodness plantings. She is a farmer that has already turned over the field and is looking for the right seeds for a bountiful harvest of new life for each of their lives.

Her bringing of God's love to each of them is purely about acceptance and self-worth. She wants them to know that the goodness of God is available to all that invite it. She invites them to invite it every time she visits. "5/22/13 ARS 8

13 - "Prison Life of the Future

The complexity of your prison systems is detrimental to many that occupy, serve, visit, and guard them. There is a palpable intensity of negativity present at most facilities.

When one can change their mind, they can change their reality. Could it be that your society could realign prison life to contain the expansion of the need for more prisons.

Unions should not worry as there is no suggestion that these places can be eliminated any time in upcoming centuries. Union leaders could help serve their members by helping the institutions become more user-friendly and economical for all.

The word economical was included to get the attention of the administrators but the goal is really to promote the lessening of dehumanization that exists within the societal dynamics from which the crop of criminals grows. The guard and others who work for institutions are exposed to the negative energy of the collected criminals and that is not exactly a nurturing vibration.

Please consider as if the vibration of a prison existed on a scale that you could read called the love fear continuum. Consider that a single increment move on that scale that went away from fear and moved towards love was actually beneficial to all who passed through the premises.

As you ever so slightly held that thought, you entertained the possibility for a shift for the imprisoned and guards of the future. Congratulations, for you have allowed some light to shine on a subject that is almost perpetually locked in pessimism." ARS 9

14 - "Prison Rehabilitation

The answer to prison rehabilitation is purpose. While some institutions may have initiated programs to engage their residents, the feeling of a purposeful life brings a new reality to the incarcerated.

Purposes to consider will be ones that work for the incarcerated as well as the society which actually pays the bills. Special characteristics to include would be the creation of a feeling of accomplishment generated by prisoner effort and drastic cost savings for the institution.

The real loss to prisons is wasted time, no productivity and no graciousness of interactive genius. If invited, the right use of time can provide different results than now seen.

There is no profit to society when cruelness is applied to the control of citizens. There may be temporary security but that comes at a big price to the potential of all.

The best way to learn about what is possible is to listen to the troubled stories of the incarcerated people. Their genius can be tapped by mining information about how to fill the gap that they slipped in to so that newer walkers on their path can find the gap filled by their charity of sharing their pain as a love patch to the sink holes of society.

The answers through this channel are coming differently than most could conceive and that is because neither you nor I have a job whose agenda has its own needs.

You ask to imagine how much can be cut from prison costs to maintain security, improve lives, create new industry and improve the focus, flavor and flair of American life and you dowsed for an answer. You got 47% reduction and you questioned your dowsing. Your questioning is wise because there is a huge industry that has roots in the status quo.

While that is true, your answer has potential that will serve the ones that would resist the initiatives that flow from the message. Their positions are survivable as is for a time unknown but their openness to change can also serve their security.

Change will happen even if they choose to use their money to resist the inevitable avalanche of change. Their opportunities are paramount in the areas of personal safety for all and the possibility to create new meaningful arrangements that are self-sustaining for all levels of the resident base and those employed in the industry." ARS 10

15 - "47% Decrease in Per Prisoner Costs

You may not be able to attain that level of decrease in your community for many reasons and that may be as your community wishes it to be. The number is suggested as a target for intellectual analysis of the extreme possibilities that would be needed to affect dramatic savings.

The rules of yesteryear need to be stretched to accommodate new thinking that will adjust to available resources. New legal structures may be needed to trade rights and privileges and new opportunities for human accomplishments.

Time is available to those behind bars and that time can do a lot to incubate new proposals when there is potential for them to be taken seriously. Frustration with interactivity between the jailed and the jailers on both sides commonly leads to a moderation of dreams so that the vibration of trust is vulnerable to extinction." ARS 11

16 - Will You Listen & Act?

I hope that I have diligently reported the perspective that I see as possible. Please write to me at ReverendMikeWanner@aol.com and let me know if I have not been clear.

The Judges and The Angel are not as free to act as you are. Americans have great power to change our world in ways that we would like.

The judges have duties and responsibilities that prevent them from having the independence that every other citizen has every day. None of us can be totally objective and subjective at the same time.

Angels do not have physical form and cannot present themselves to the political system and suggest changes to the way things work. You have physical form and can present yourself to the political system and suggest changes to the way things work.

BUT BUT BUT and more BUTs. You are totally at choice and you know specifics.

Secondarily, if you have gotten this far in this book then it is likely that you have a reason to create change because the way things are is a major stressor in your life.

Your power to make change is subtle and powerful. You can make success instead or processing stress. You will enjoy every little bit of success that you create and that will motivate you.

17 - What Can You Do?

1. Tune in to the Divine Channel of possibility through Prayer.

2. Tune up your awareness to the 501C3 organizations that speak the message that you want the world to hear.

3. Make a time donation to a 501C3 Organization that you like.

4. Sign up for e-mail or other mailing lists that keep you up to date with the aspects of the system that you want changed most.

5. Make a donation to the top 501C3 Organization that you like.

6. Become politically aware of candidates who suggest change.

7. Consider volunteering for causes you would like to see succeed.

What's Next Is Up To You!

God Bless You!

Mike

For
Considering
These
Ideas

Ever

It Does Not Help Prayer Still Does!

Resource Site http://www.Create-A-Prayer.com

20 - Resource Books

Distant Healing Sessions (or Join Mail List) – Write To mikewann@voicenet.com

Books by Rev. Mike at www.Amazon.com

Veterans Healing Six Pack
1. *Trauma Healing Options for VA Hospitals: Help for Veterans to Own Their Healing and their future.*
2. *Trauma Healing Action Steps for Veterans: Help to Start Healing*
3. *Trauma Healing Action Steps for Veterans: Empowerment*
4. *Trauma Healing Action Steps for Veterans: Forgiveness*
5. *Trauma Healing Action Steps for Veterans: Thought Freedom*
6. *Tea For Veterans: Welcome One Home*

PTSD Power Pack:
1. *The PTSD Project: Turn Pain To Power*
2. *PTSD & Soul Retrieval: Putting One Back Together*
3. *PTSD & The Purple PAD: Calling all Scientists and PTSD Patients*

Angel Raphael Speaks Volume 1: Take Courage! God Has Healing in Store for You!
Angel Raphael Speaks Volume 2: Take Courage! God Has Healing in Store for You!
Angel Raphael Speaks Volume 3: Take Courage! God Has Healing in Store for You!
Angel Raphael Speaks Volume 4: Angels, Addicts, Alcoholics & Prisoners – Oh Yeah!
Angel Raphael Speaks Volume 5: Prisoners Caring for Alcoholics - Australia In Miniature Projects Intro
Angel Raphael Speaks Volume 6: Prisoners Caring for Addicts - Australia In Miniature For Addicts
Reiki Journaling from Japan
Reiki Is Alive: God's Great Gift
Four Parts to Healing
Distant Healing: We Are All Connected
Stress Release Energy Work: How To Cope
Does Reiki Love Heal Cancer?
Group Consciousness
Salute To Philadelphia VA Medical Center: Thank You
Reiki Transcript for Reiki 2 & 3 Channels: Dr. Usui Is That You?
God Bless Kindle & Amazon
Puppies Are Different From People
If Your Dog Dies
Toy Guns Are Obsolete
Great Spirit Made Children With Red Skin: AND

The Cage of Fear: Is Not Locked
God Made Children Red, Yellow, Brown, Black & White: Greet Each Child With Kindness
Emergency Medical Kindness In The Cradle Of Liberty: Big City - Cracked Bell
Angels Are Always Around Addicts and Addicts: Help Is Near Now! Invite It In!
Angels Are Always Around Addicts and Alcoholics: Volume 2 - Tools To Help Re-Light Your Life
Prison Jobs Now: Providing Care For Addicts And Addicts
Controlled Care Communities Concept
Prison Possibilities Dialogue Series: Concept
Prison Possibilities Dialogue Series: Volume 2, 3, 4, 5 Dialogues
Prison Possibilities Voluntary Exile
Prison Possibilities Corrections Coaches
Prison Possibilities For Mexicans: Is A Boat Better Than A Wall?
Prison Possibilities Family Time: A Reason to Thrive!
Prison Genius Pool: "So Much Genius In Jail"
Prison Possibilities Access Control: Prisoner Access by Request
Prisoner's Lawyers Can Save The American Economy: Make A Buck Doing It & Be Thanked!
Prisoner Family Talks, Days, Stays & Vacations: Connecting Helps Healing
Prisoner Writing Projects: Write To Heal, Start Over & Reconnect
Prison Cell Clearing & Blessing: Clear Entities, Chase Ghosts, and & Create Sacred Space
Prison Reiki? Maybe Someday? A Gateway To Help Heal Prisons & America?

Little Books at Kindle.com by Rev. Mike:
English Medical History Questionnaire For Non-English Speakers
English Language Helper For Non-English Speakers
Wise Wonderful Women Are The Well Of The Family
Answers for Test & Research: Dowsing Power
Crisis? Reiki! Baby? Reiki!
Bible References For Healing
Angel Raphael Speaks – Prisons
Angel Raphael Speaks – Veterans
The Saint Off Interstate 95

Angel Raphael Speaks through Rev. Mike Wanner. Please visit
http://www.AngelRaphaelSpeaks.com

21 - Angels Please Prayers

Addict's

Angels of Healing Selected
Help Me to Stay Directed
Come To Me From The Sky
I Am Ready to Succeed Not Try
If I Don't Invite You In
I Might Not Win
I Have Been Lost For Too Long
Help Me To Stay Strong

Alcoholic's

Angels of Healing On High
Help Me to Stay Dry
Come To Me From The Sky
I Am Ready to Succeed Not Try
If I Don't Invite You In
I Might Not Win
I Have Been Lost For Too Long
Help Me To Stay Strong

From

http://AngelRaphaelSpeaks.com/AAAAAAA/

22 - Private Channeling

Angel Raphael Speaks is a series of free messages that are channeled through Reverend Mike Wanner for the Highest good and Highest Healing of all concerned.

Many questions arise about Reverend Mike doing private channeling and he does help with that so e-mail him.

Reverend Mike is available world-wide as a psychic channel, emotional release facilitator, spiritual energy practitioner & teacher, and public speaker. He looks forward to meeting you soon!

Email - mikewann@voicenet.com   215-342-1270 PRIVATE SPIRITUAL READINGS/channelings or Spiritual Healing Sessions: Telephone or in person. Rev. Mike is available for private, one-on-one intuitive sessions with you, his Guide Family, and your Guides. He helps by offering clarity on emotional situations about your life, your purpose, your spirituality, and the release of stuffed emotions and cellular memory.

Connect to the love of your Guides today!
Contact Rev. Mike for an appointment.
Sessions available:

Spiritual Readings
Angel Channeling
Distant Reiki Healing
Distant Clearing of Stuffed Emotions
Distant Clearing Cellular Memory
Distant Clearing Energy Blockages
Distant Clearing of the Chakras
Customized needs
Mastermind dowsing responses to yes/no direction finding questions.

Rev. Mike is a facilitator of healing. He brings you and the Divine together so that you can align with the Divine and have a great time and a great life. All healing is between you and God, as it should be. Go ahead and start without Rev. Mike. Visit his prayer site http://www.Create-A-Prayer.com. Take the first step NOW.

23 - Reverend Mike Wanner

Rev. Mike Wanner started his metaphysical and ministerial studies with Reiki in 1993 and has studied seven styles of Reiki in the U.S., Japan, Canada, Denmark and Australia. He is certified to teach. He became certified to teach Integrated Energy Therapy in 1999 and co-taught the first IET class of the new Millennium. Mike began dowsing in 2001.

Ordained as a Metaphysical Minister of the International Metaphysical Ministry and an Interfaith Minister of the Circle of Miracles Ministry, Rev. Mike practices and teaches spiritual energy therapies in the Philadelphia Area.

Rev. Mike holds ministerial degrees from the University of Metaphysics and the University of Sedona. He is a Pastoral Care Associate of Aria - Frankford Hospital. He taught at the National Academy of Massage Therapy and Health Sciences.

Rev. Mike was a faculty member of the Medical Mission Sister's Center for Human Integration's School of Integrated Body/Mind Therapies in Fox Chase, Philadelphia, PA for twelve years.

Rev. Mike is licensed by the teaching of Intuitional Metaphysics to practice Spiritual Healing and Scientific Prayer. Mike is also a Prayer therapist.

Rev. Mike was elected in 2007 to the status of "Fellow of the American Institute of Stress."

In 2008, Rev. Mike became a practitioner of Coincidental Recognition as he incorporated the CoRe System in to his spiritual healing practice.

In 2009, Rev. Mike trademarked a new healing process called Quantum Quatro! Subtle Energy System Support®.

In 2011, Rev. Mike joined the outreach program known as the Health Advantage Group.

In 2012, Rev. Mike became a Certified Professional Coach by The Master Coaching Academy and Joined the Personal Empowerment Group.

Prior to his metaphysical, ministerial and coaching studies, Rev. Mike worked for Sears Roebuck and Co. while in High School and after graduation until he joined the U. S. Air Force in 1965. He returned to Sears from Vietnam in 1969 and stayed until 1978. His final Sears assignment was as an efficiency expert in Methods - Operational Research and Development.

He volunteered with Burholme Emergency Medical Services from 1969 and is still a Life Member and Board of Directors Member. He started a private ambulance company in 1975 and worked professionally in the field until 2001 when he devoted his full attention to real estate investing, healing, coaching and writing.

www.ReverendMikeWanner.com

www.ingramcontent.com/pod-product-compliance
Lightning Source LLC
Chambersburg PA
CBHW051420170526
45165CB00004BA/1895